How To Build The Rugby Player Body;
Building a Rugby Player Physique, The Rugby Player Workout

By

M Laurence

Table of Contents

1. The plan to Build the Body
2. Old Exercises - New Tricks
3. Monday - Training - Chest and Back
4. Monday - Nutrition
5. Tuesday - Training - Biceps, Triceps and Shoulders
6. Tuesday - Nutrition
7. Wednesday - Legs and Calves
8. Wednesday - Nutrition
9. Thursday - Chest and Back
10. Thursday - Nutrition
11. Friday - Biceps, Triceps and Shoulders
12. Friday - Nutrition
13. Saturday - Legs and Calves
14. Saturday - Nutrition
15. Sunday - Rest and Recover
16. Monday Week 2 - Back and Biceps
17. Monday Week 2 - Nutrition
18. Tuesday Week 2 - Abs and Rest
19. Wednesday Week 2 - Chest and Triceps
20. Wednesday Week 2 - Nutrition
21. Thursday Week 2 - Abs and Rest
22. Friday Week 2 - Legs and Calves
23. Friday Week 2 - Nutrition
24. Saturday Week 2 - Abs and Rest
25. Sunday - Rest
26. Final Notes and Cheats

1. The plan to Build the Body

Many people watched the rugby world cup and admired the physiques on show -an incredible mix of power, strength and athleticism.

It's the aesthetics the powerful legs, big arms, huge chest, wide back all tapering to and perhaps the most important - a tight flat stomach.

The great thing about a rugby player body is they are achievable, they aren't some freak of nature with ludicrous conditioning. You can achieve it if you put the work in. I'm going to give you a balls-to-the wall workout routine to get this physique.

To give you a quick overview of how we will achieve this i have broken the training regime down into 3 areas:

1 - Training Frequency
Many people say you can only train a body part once a week. This is theory is fast becoming outdated. As usual all we have to do is look to the past. Did you know many of the 60's and 70's bodybuilders were training the entire body 2-3 times a week. 3 times a week is extreme for a normal person who has work and earn a living etc So like me you want something high impact, time friendly and results driven. So the regime is spread over two weeks, training the body twice in the first week and once in the second. And repeat.

2 - Body Fat
There's a number of thinks you need to consider to get the maximum out of your workouts. Your Testosterone is utilized at its best when you have a lower body fat percentage. So this is the number one issue to deal with

when beginning a new regime. A low body fat percentage gives you more utilization. This is also why the workouts are supersets. We are ramping up your intensity and effort to burn additional calories.

3 - Nutrition
Nutrition is considered the most important part of building muscle. If the nutrition is incorrect then it doesn't matter how impeccable your training routines are, you will not progress. I'm sure you have an idea about nutrition, but I'm here to give your knowledge a little boast. You've heard of high protein, carbohydrates and healthy fats? But what is the most effective foods to eat to get those essential nutrients. This equals feeding your muscles exactly what they need and therefore means you will build muscle. Last but not least is a high water intake, this cleans our systems, regulates body temperature and keeps the entire body hydrated. So with heavy exercise, 3 litres a day is an ideal figure to aim for.

2. Old Exercises - New Tricks

1 Week hard-core - 1 week hard

So as I've already said this is a two week workout and repeat. Week 1 you will train the whole body twice, everyday two body parts and rest Sunday. This will shock the muscles into growth. The additional work-load will blast the muscles into adjusting and therefore grow. The second week reverts to training the whole body once. This is probably what you have been doing? This allows the muscles to recover, grow, and replenish their energy stores. Yet we still hit them just to keep them guessing and working.

Supersets to Size

Supersets are time-efficient. By doing sets back-to-back, you reduce your total workout time while still doing the same amount of total work.
Supersetting is fantastic for pummelling antagonistic muscles - Back/Chest and Biceps/Triceps and legs Hams/Glutes. Supersets increase Lactic Acid production, which helps boost Growth Hormone (GH) levels in the body. The body responds to the reduced pH (increased acidity) in the body from the production of Lactic Acid by secreting GH. GH is a powerful fat loss and muscle building hormone.

Power and Intensity

We will be building more explosive power which will therefore build strength faster. This is done using tempo. By this i mean a 1 second pull/push/ on a given move - POWERFUL and with FORCE - and then under perfect control a 4 second release. The muscles are still working all the way. So we are changing the tempo, the speed of either the concentric (shortening) or eccentric (lengthening) component of the lift. There is no 'resting' at the bottom of any move. As soon as you are as close to the bottom of the move - you POWER back up for the 1 second concentric and again release for 4 second eccentric under your complete control. This should give you a great pump and be a challenge to start with.

Why?
You must have heard of the term TUT - Time Under Tension - there are a number of variations on the term, they all mean the same. You may find that you're actually only working your muscles for 5 minutes in an hour workout! With the 1 second concentric and 4 second eccentric move with no rest we work the muscle much harder for longer.
Many people will struggle with this at first as it's so common to do one arm curl, take a break/release all tension and do another. Even a split second rest is still a release of tension. Not good enough. You need to be working your muscles 100% of the time during a set. THEN you rest between sets. You will do more damage to the muscle and get better results to stimulate growth.

So let's get to it.

3. Monday - Training - Chest and Back

Cardio - A.M
Before breakfast go for a 25minute run. This burns fat straightaway and gets your metabolism fired up.

Weights:
I like my heavy workout first thing in the morning. If this is the case for you as well you need fuel before you go, something fast digesting: a 25gram protein shake, a banana and a handful of granola prior to a workout. If you do weights first thing in the morning move your cardio to before dinner later on.

The exercises are split into two exercises per round performed one set after another. Rest time is 45 seconds per set. So at 30 seconds the weights should be back in your hand. Keep water with a scoop of BCAA's handy.

Round 1

Increase the weight little by little with each set.

Exercise	Sets/Reps
BARBELL BENCH PRESS - MEDIUM GRIP	1-2 sets of 15 reps (warm-up); 5 sets of 12, 10, 8, 6, 4 reps
Superset	
CHIN-UP	5 sets of 15, 12, 10, 8, 8 reps

Round 2

Increase the weight little by little with each set.

Exercise	Sets/Reps
BARBELL INCLINE BENCH PRESS	5 sets of 12, 10, 8, 6, 4 reps
Superset	
WIDE-GRIP REAR PULL-UP	5 sets of 15, 12, 10, 8, 8 reps

Round 3

Increase the weight little by little with each set.

Exercise	Sets/Reps
DUMBBELL FLYES	4 sets of 12, 10, 8, 6 reps
Superset	
T-BAR ROW	4 sets of 15, 12, 8, 6 reps

4. Monday - Nutrition

We are aiming for around 1 gram of protein for 1 pound of body weight to give your muscles the fuel to grow. For example:

A person weighing 176bls / 80kg you would aim for 176grams of protein.

This is relatively high. However protein shakes can add easy grams of protein to your diet. Now this is a guide. You might try this and after a few weeks feel you're not getting enough. In which case you could add a further 50 grams of protein to your diet through two smaller meals, an extra protein shake or simply making your meals a little larger. Some nutritionists even recommend 1.5-2 grams of protein to 1 pound of bodyweight.
So the person weighing 176 would eat 264 (1.5grams of protein) or 353 (2 grams of protein)

The emphasis is on continuous supply of nutrients - protein and fat. Carbs are placed at the start of the day - in among your training ideally. You ideally don't want any carbs after lunch.

Ultimately you will have to experiment. So let's get to it.

Meal One

1 x multivitamin
3-4 Whole Eggs
Bacon/Sausages or Quorn

Oats
1/4 cup with 1 tbsp. honey
NUTRITION FACTS

Calories: 561   Fat: 30.4 g   Carbs: 16.2 g   Protein: 22.1 g

Meal Two

2 Scoops of a 25 gram protein Whey Isolate shake

NUTRITION FACTS
Calories: 230   Fat: 20 g   Carbs: 10 g   Protein: 50 g

Meal Three

Grilled Lean Beef
12 ounces

Vegetables
1-2 cups
NUTRITION FACTS
Calories: 638   Fat: 29 g   Carbs: 63 g   Protein: 48 g

Meal Four

Full-Fat Cottage Cheese
2 cups
Almonds and Cashews
2 ounces

NUTRITION FACTS
Calories: 752   Fat: 34 g Carb: 18 g   Protein: 52 g

The Total Protein intake is 172 grams of protein. I would have 2 scoops of protein after your workout, plus Creatine making a grand total of 221.

This is a figure you can play with, add more, take away some etc

5. Tuesday - Training - Biceps, Triceps and Shoulders

Cardio - A.M
Before breakfast go for a 25minute run. This burns fat straightaway and gets your metabolism fired up.

Weights:
As I've said fuel before you go, something fast digesting: a 25gram protein shake, a banana and a handful of granola prior to a workout. If you do weights first thing in the morning move your cardio to before dinner.

The exercises are split into two exercises per round performed one set after another. Rest time is 45 seconds per set. So at 30 seconds the weights should be back in your hand.

Round 1

Increase the weight little by little with each set.

Exercise	Sets/Reps
SEATED BARBELL MILITARY PRESS	4 sets of 12, 10, 10, 8 reps
Superset	
BARBELL CURL	4 sets of 10-12 reps
Superset	
LYING TRICEPS PRESS	4 sets of 10-12 reps

Round 2

Increase the weight little by little with each set.

Exercise	Sets/Reps
SIDE LATERAL RAISE	4 sets of 12, 12, 10, 8 reps
Superset	
DUMBBELL ALTERNATE BICEP CURL	4 sets of 10-12 reps
Superset	
TRICEPS PUSHDOWN	4 sets of 10-12 reps

Round 3

Increase the weight little by little with each set.

Exercise	Sets/Reps
SMITH MACHINE OVERHEAD SHOULDER PRESS	4 sets of 12, 10, 10, 8 reps
Superset	
INCLINE DUMBBELL CURL	4 sets of 10-12 rep
Superset	
CABLE ROPE OVERHEAD TRICEPS EXTENSION	4 sets of 10-12 reps

6. Tuesday - Nutrition

Meal One

1 x multivitamin

1 Whey Protein shake - with peanut butter and a banana

Bowl of Granola
NUTRITION FACTS
Calories: 561   Fat: 30.4 g   Carbs: 16.2 g   Protein: 28 g

Meal Two

2 Scoops of a 25 gram protein Whey Isolate shake

NUTRITION FACTS
Calories: 230   Fat: 20 g   Carbs: 10 g   Protein: 50 g

Meal Three

Two tins of Tuna
10 ounces

Vegetables/salad
1 cup
NUTRITION FACTS
Calories: 771   Fat: 33.2 g   Carbs: 17 g   Protein: 58 g

Meal Four

High Protein Yogurt
2 cups

NUTRITION FACTS
Calories: 752   Fat: 34 g Carb: 18 g   Protein: 52 g

The Total Protein intake is 182 grams of protein. I would have 2 scoops of protein plus Creatine after your workout making a grand total of 239.

This is a figure you can play with, add more, take away some etc

7. Wednesday - Legs and Calves

With the other workouts i superset two moves and this saves time and creates a cardio effect, while allowing you to hit two body parts hard. However with legs which are a very large body part and demand heavy workouts I do one exercise at a time. Also remember your limits with heavy weight. It is much better to master your form for Squats with a lighter weight. Let your muscles get used to the heavy weight gradually.

Cardio - A.M
Before breakfast go for a 25minute run. This burns fat straightaway and gets your metabolism fired up.

Weights:
Again if training first thing: a 25gram protein shake, a banana and a handful of granola prior to a workout. If you do weights first thing in the morning move your cardio to before dinner.

Rest time is 45 seconds per set. So at 30 seconds the weights should be back in your hand.

Round 1

Increase the weight little by little with each set.

Exercise	Sets/Reps
SQUAT	1-2 sets of 15 reps (warm-up); 5 sets of 12, 10, 8, 6, 4 reps
LEG EXTENSIONS	5 sets of 15, 12, 10, 8, 8 reps
LYING LEG CURLS	4 sets of 10 reps

Round 2

Increase the weight little by little with each set.

Exercise	Sets/Reps
BARBELL SQUAT	5 sets of 12, 10, 8, 6, 4 reps
STANDING LEG CURL	5 sets of 15, 12, 10, 8, 8 reps
SMITH MACHINE LEG PRESS	4 sets of 8 reps

Round 3

Increase the weight little by little with each set.

Exercise	Sets/Reps
STANDING CALF RAISES	5 sets of 12, 10, 8, 6, 4 reps
SEATED CALF RAISE	4 sets of 12-15 reps

8. Wednesday - Nutrition

Meal One

3-4 Whole Eggs Boiled
Bacon/Sausages or Quorn

Oats
1/4 cup with 1 tbsp. honey
NUTRITION FACTS
Calories: 561   Fat: 30.4 g   Carbs: 16.2 g   Protein: 22.1 g

Meal Two

2 Scoops of 25 gram protein Whey Isolate shake

NUTRITION FACTS
Calories: 230   Fat: 20 g   Carbs: 10 g   Protein: 50 g

Meal Three

Chicken Breast pieces
10 ounces

Vegetables
1 cup
NUTRITION FACTS
Calories: 771   Fat: 33.2 g   Carbs: 17 g   Protein: 58 g

Meal Four

Full-Fat Cottage Cheese
2 cups
Cashews
2 ounces

NUTRITION FACTS
Calories: 752   Fat: 34 g Carb: 18 g   Protein: 52 g

The Total Protein intake is 182 grams of protein. I would have 2 scoops of protein after your workout making a grand total of 231.

This is a figure you can play with, add more, take away some etc.

9. Thursday - Chest and Back

Okay we will be hitting the back and chest with different exercises and just taxing the muscles in different ways to keep them guessing. We don't want to slip into a routine. Then your progress will slow.

Cardio - A.M
Before breakfast go for a 25minute run. This burns fat straightaway and gets your metabolism fired up.

Weights:
Morning workout: a 25gram protein shake, a banana and a handful of granola prior to a workout. If you do weights first thing in the morning move your cardio to before dinner.

The exercises are split into two exercises per round performed one set after another. Rest time is 45 seconds per set. So at 30 seconds the weights should be back in your hand.

Round 1

Increase the weight little by little with each set.

Exercise	Sets/Reps
BARBELL DECLINE BENCH PRESS - MEDIUM GRIP	4 sets of 12, 10, 8, 6 reps
Superset BARBELL ROWS	4 sets of 12, 12, 10, 10 reps

Round 2

Increase the weight little by little with each set.

Exercise	Sets/Reps
DUMB BELL BENCH PRESS -	4 sets of 12, 10, 8, 6 reps
Superset	
NARROW-GRIP REAR PULL-UP	4 sets of 15, 12, 10, 8 reps

Round 3

Increase the weight little by little with each set.

Exercise	Sets/Reps
DUMBBELL FLYES	3 sets of 12, 10, 8 reps
Superset	
ONE ARM ROWS	3 sets of 15, 12, 8 reps

10. Thursday - Nutrition

Meal One

1 x multivitamin
6 Scrambled Whole Eggs

Oats
1/4 cup with 1 tbsp. honey

NUTRITION FACTS
Calories: 561   Fat: 30.4 g Carbs: 16.2 g   Protein: 40.1g

Meal Two

2 Scoops of 25 gram protein Whey Isolate shake

NUTRITION FACTS
Calories: 230   Fat: 20 g   Carbs: 10 g   Protein: 50 g

Meal Three

Grilled Fish/Red Meat
10 ounces

Brussels Sprouts
1 cup

NUTRITION FACTS
Calories: 771   Fat: 33.2 g   Carbs: 17 g   Protein: 58 g

Meal Four

High Protein Yogurt
2 cups

NUTRITION FACTS
Calories: 752   Fat: 34 g Carb: 18 g   Protein: 52 g

The Total Protein intake is 182 grams of protein. I would have 2 scoops of protein plus creatine after your workout making a grand total of 251.

This is a figure you can play with, add more, take away some etc.

11. Friday - Biceps, Triceps and Shoulders

This being the second workout of the week we are hitting different muscles and attacking them using less sets.

Cardio - A.M
Before breakfast go for a 25minute run. This burns fat straightaway and gets your metabolism fired up.

Weights:
Morning workout: a 25gram protein shake, a banana and a handful of granola prior to a workout. If you do weights first thing in the morning move your cardio to before dinner.

The exercises are split into two exercises per round performed one set after another. Rest time is 45 seconds per set. So at 30 seconds the weights should be back in your hand.

Round 1

Increase the weight little by little with each set.

Exercise	Sets/Reps
DUMBBELL SHOULDER PRESS	1-2 sets of 15 reps (warm-up); 4 sets of 12, 10, 10, 8 reps
Superset	
INCLINE DUMBBELL CURL	4 sets of 10-12 reps
Superset	
LYING TRICEPS EXTENSION	4 sets of 10-12 reps

Round 2

Increase the weight little by little with each set.

Exercise	Sets/Reps
LATERAL RAISE	4 sets of 12, 10, 8, 6 reps
Superset	
HAMMER CURLS	4 sets of 15, 12, 10, 8 reps
Superset	
CABLE ROPE OVERHEAD TRICEPS EXTENSION	4 sets of 10-12 reps

Round 3

Increase the weight little by little with each set.

Exercise	Sets/Reps
BENT OVER RAISES	3 sets of 12, 10, 8 reps
Superset	
REVERSE GRIP CURLS - EZ BAR	3 sets of 15, 12, 8 reps
Superset	
DUMBBELL ONE-ARM TRICEPS EXTENSION	3 sets of 15, 12, 8 reps

12. Friday - Nutrition

Meal One

1 x multivitamin
3-4 Whole Eggs
Bacon/Sausages or Quorn

Oats
1/4 cup with 1 tbsp. honey
NUTRITION FACTS
Calories: 561   Fat: 30.4 g   Carbs: 16.2 g   Protein: 22.1
g

Meal Two

2 Scoops of 25 gram protein Whey Isolate shake

NUTRITION FACTS
Calories: 230   Fat: 20 g   Carbs: 10 g   Protein: 50 g

Meal Three

Salmon
10 ounces

Steamed Broccoli
1 cup

NUTRITION FACTS
Calories: 771   Fat: 33.2 g   Carbs: 17 g   Protein: 58 g

Meal Four

2 scoops Casine Protein shake with Soya Milk

NUTRITION FACTS
Calories: 752   Fat: 34 g Carb: 18 g   Protein: 52 g

The Total Protein intake is 182 grams of protein. I would have 2 scoops of protein plus creatine after your workout making a grand total of 231.

This is a figure you can play with, add more, take away some etc.

13. Saturday - Legs and Calves

Here is the second workout of the week, still hard and heavy but less sets. The legs will have recovered since the last workout and now need another hit. But by reducing the amount of sets they will be ready for the next workout which is bigger.

Cardio - A.M
Before breakfast go for a 25minute run. This burns fat straightaway and gets your metabolism fired up.

Weights:
The exercises are split into two exercises per round performed one set after another. Rest time is 45 seconds per set. So at 30 seconds the weights should be back in your hand.

Round 1

Increase the weight little by little with each set.

Exercise	Sets/Reps
BARBELL SQUAT	2 warm up light sets, 4 sets of 12, 10, 8, 8 reps
STANDING LEG CURL	4 sets of 15, 12, 10, 8 reps
SMITH MACHINE LEG PRESS	4 sets of 8 reps

Round 2

Increase the weight little by little with each set.

Exercise	Sets/Reps
DEADLIFT	3 sets of 12, 10, 8 reps
LEG EXTENSIONS	3 sets of 15, 12, 10 reps
LEG CURLS	3 sets of 10 reps

Round 3

Increase the weight little by little with each set.

Exercise	Sets/Reps
STANDING CALF RAISES	3 sets of 12, 10, 8 reps
SEATED CALF RAISE	3 sets of 12-15 reps

14. Saturday - Nutrition

Meal One

1 x multivitamin
2 Whole Eggs
1 piece of salmon

Oats
1/4 cup with 1 tbsp honey
NUTRITION FACTS
Calories: 561   Fat: 30.4 g Carbs: 16.2 g   Protein: 30.1g

Meal Two

2 Scoops of 25 gram protein Whey Isolate shake

NUTRITION FACTS
Calories: 230   Fat: 20 g   Carbs: 10 g   Protein: 50 g

Meal Three

Quorn Burgers
10 ounces

Peas and Carrots
1 cup
NUTRITION FACTS
Calories: 771   Fat: 33.2 g   Carbs: 17 g   Protein: 58 g

Meal Four

Full-Fat Cottage Cheese
2 cups
Handful of Pumpkin seeds

NUTRITION FACTS
Calories: 752   Fat: 34 g Carb: 18 g   Protein: 42 g

The Total Protein intake is 172 grams of protein. I would have 2 scoops of protein plus creatine after your workout making a grand total of 231.

This is a figure you can play with, add more, take away some etc.

15. Sunday - Rest and Recover

So we've made it to our rest day - well done for an epic week of workouts!

So today is all about chilling, eating well, having your cheat meal - which is anything of your choice.

Meal One

1 x multivitamin
3-4 Whole Eggs
Bacon/Sausages or Quorn

Oats
1/4 cup with 1 tbsp. honey
NUTRITION FACTS
Calories: 561   Fat: 30.4 g   Carbs: 16.2 g   Protein: 22.1 g

Meal Two

2 Scoops of a 25 gram protein Whey Isolate shake

NUTRITION FACTS
Calories: 230   Fat: 20 g   Carbs: 10 g   Protein: 50 g

Meal Three

Cheat Meal!

Meal Four

Soya Yogurt
2 cups
Cashews
2 ounces

NUTRITION FACTS
Calories: 752   Fat: 29 g Carb: 16 g   Protein: 45 g

16. Monday Week 2 - Back and Biceps

Week two begins and let's start as we mean to finish - let's go.

Round 1

Increase the weight little by little with each set.

Exercise	Sets/Reps
CHIN-UP	1-2 sets of 15 reps (warm-up); 5 sets of 12, 10, 8, 6, 4 reps
Superset	
BARBELL CURL	4 sets of 10-12 reps

Round 2

Increase the weight little by little with each set.

Exercise	Sets/Reps
WIDE-GRIP REAR PULL-UP	5 sets of 15, 12, 10, 8, 8 reps
Superset	
DUMBBELL ALTERNATE BICEP CURL	4 sets of 10-12 reps

Round 3

Increase the weight little by little with each set.

Exercise	Sets/Reps
T-BAR ROW	4 sets of 15, 12, 8, 6 reps
Superset	
INCLINE DUMBBELL CURL	4 sets of 10-12 rep

17. Monday Week 2 - Nutrition

Meal One

1 x multivitamin
3-4 Whole Eggs
Bacon/Sausages or Quorn

Oats
1/4 cup with 1 tbsp. honey

NUTRITION FACTS
Calories: 561   Fat: 30.4 g Carbs: 16.2 g   Protein: 22.1g

Meal Two

2 Scoops of 25 gram protein Whey Isolate shake

NUTRITION FACTS
Calories: 230   Fat: 20 g   Carbs: 10 g   Protein: 50 g

Meal Three

2 Burger Patties
10 ounces

Broccoli, Carrots
1 cup

NUTRITION FACTS
Calories: 771   Fat: 33.2 g   Carbs: 17 g   Protein: 58 g

Meal Four

Full-Fat Cottage Cheese

2 cups
Cashews
2 ounces

NUTRITION FACTS
Calories: 752   Fat: 34 g Carb: 18 g   Protein: 52 g

The Total Protein intake is 182 grams of protein. I would have 2 scoops of protein plus creatine after your workout making a grand total of 231.

This is a figure you can play with, add more, take away some etc

18. Tuesday Week 2 - Abs and Rest

Before Breakfast:
20 x Crunches x 3
25 twists x 3 each side

Meal One

3-4 Whole Eggs Boiled
Bacon/Sausages or Quorn

Oats
1/4 cup with 1 tbsp honey

NUTRITION FACTS
Calories: 561   Fat: 30.4 g   Carbs: 16.2 g   Protein: 22.1 g

Meal Two

2 Scoops of 25 gram protein Whey Isolate shake

NUTRITION FACTS
Calories: 230   Fat: 20 g   Carbs: 10 g   Protein: 50 g

Meal Three

Chicken Breasts
10 ounces

Rocket and sliced beetroot
1 cup

NUTRITION FACTS
Calories: 771   Fat: 33.2 g   Carbs: 17 g   Protein: 58 g

Meal Four

2 Scoops of Casein Protein with Almond Milk

NUTRITION FACTS
Calories: 752   Fat: 34 g Carb: 18 g   Protein: 42 g

The Total Protein intake is 172 grams of protein. I would have 2 scoops of protein after your workout making a grand total of 221.

This is a figure you can play with, add more, take away some etc.

19. Wednesday Week 2 - Chest and Triceps

Round 1

Increase the weight little by little with each set.

Exercise	Sets/Reps
BARBELL BENCH PRESS - MEDIUM GRIP	1-2 sets of 15 reps (warm-up); 5 sets of 12, 10, 8, 6, 4 reps
Superset	
LYING TRICEPS PRESS	5 sets of 15, 12, 10, 8, 8 reps

Round 2

Increase the weight little by little with each set.

Exercise	Sets/Reps
BARBELL INCLINE BENCH PRESS	5 sets of 12, 10, 8, 6, 4 reps
Superset	
TRICEPS PUSHDOWN	5 sets of 15, 12, 10, 8, 8 reps

Round 3

Increase the weight little by little with each set.

Exercise	Sets/Reps
DUMBBELL FLYES	4 sets of 12, 10, 8, 6 reps
Superset	
CABLE ROPE OVERHEAD TRICEPS EXTENSION	4 sets of 15, 12, 8, 6 reps

20. Wednesday Week 2 - Nutrition

Meal One

1 x multivitamin

1 Whey Protein shake - with peanut butter and a banana

Bowl of Granola

NUTRITION FACTS
Calories: 561   Fat: 30.4 g   Carbs: 16.2 g   Protein: 28 g

Meal Two

2 Scoops of 25 gram protein Whey Isolate shake

NUTRITION FACTS
Calories: 230   Fat: 20 g   Carbs: 10 g   Protein: 50 g

Meal Three

Two tins of Tuna
10 ounces

Beetroot and diced Carrots
1 cup

NUTRITION FACTS
Calories: 771   Fat: 33.2 g   Carbs: 17 g   Protein: 58 g

Meal Four

High Protein Yogurt
2 cups
Almonds
2 ounces

NUTRITION FACTS
Calories: 752   Fat: 34 g Carb: 18 g   Protein: 50 g

The Total Protein intake is 180 grams of protein. I would have 2 scoops of protein plus Creatine after your workout making a grand total of 237.

This is a figure you can play with, add more, take away some etc

21. Thursday Week 2 - Abs and Rest

Before Breakfast:
20 x Crunches x 3
25 twists x 3 each side

Meal One

1 x multivitamin
2 Whole Eggs
1 piece of salmon

Oats
1/4 cup with 1 tbsp. honey

NUTRITION FACTS
Calories: 561   Fat: 30.4 g   Carbs: 16.2 g   Protein: 30.1g

Meal Two

2 Scoops of 25 gram protein Whey Isolate shake

NUTRITION FACTS
Calories: 230   Fat: 20 g   Carbs: 10 g   Protein: 50 g

Meal Three

Grilled Cod
10 ounces

Spouts, Cabbage and green beans
1 cup
NUTRITION FACTS
Calories: 771   Fat: 33.2 g   Carbs: 17 g   Protein: 58 g

Meal Four

Full-Fat Cottage Cheese
2 cups
Almonds, Walnuts, or Cashews
2 ounces

NUTRITION FACTS
Calories: 752   Fat: 34 g Carb: 18 g   Protein: 52 g

The Total Protein intake is 182 grams of protein. I would have 2 scoops of protein plus creatine after your workout making a grand total of 241.

This is a figure you can play with, add more, take away some etc

22. Friday Week 2 - Legs and Calves

Round 1

Increase the weight little by little with each set.

Exercise	Sets/Reps
BARBELL SQUAT	2 warm up light sets, 4 sets of 12, 10, 8, 8 reps
STANDING LEG CURL	4 sets of 15, 12, 10, 8 reps
SMITH MACHINE LEG PRESS	4 sets of 8 reps

Round 2

Increase the weight little by little with each set.

Exercise	Sets/Reps
DEADLIFT	3 sets of 12, 10, 8 reps
LEG EXTENSIONS	3 sets of 15, 12, 10 reps
LEG CURLS	3 sets of 10 reps

Round 3

Increase the weight little by little with each set.

Exercise	Sets/Reps
STANDING CALF RAISES	3 sets of 12, 10, 8 reps
SEATED CALF RAISE	3 sets of 12-15 reps

23. Friday Week 2 - Nutrition

Meal One

1 x multivitamin
6 Scrambled Whole Eggs

Oats
1/4 cup with 1 tbsp. honey
NUTRITION FACTS
Calories: 561   Fat: 30.4 g   Carbs: 16.2 g   Protein: 40.1
g

Meal Two

2 Scoops of 25 gram protein Whey Isolate shake

NUTRITION FACTS
Calories: 230   Fat: 20 g   Carbs: 10 g   Protein: 50 g

Meal Three

2 Burger Patties
10 ounces

Beetroot, Carrots and Rocket
1 cup

NUTRITION FACTS
Calories: 771   Fat: 33.2 g   Carbs: 17 g   Protein: 58 g

Meal Four

Full-Fat Cottage Cheese
2 cups
Pumpkin Seeds
2 ounces

NUTRITION FACTS
Calories: 752   Fat: 34 g Carb: 18 g   Protein: 52 g

The Total Protein intake is 182 grams of protein. I would have 2 scoops of protein plus creatine after your workout making a grand total of 251.

This is a figure you can play with, add more, take away some etc

24. Saturday Week 2 - Abs and Rest

Before Breakfast:
20 x Crunches x 3
25 twists x 3 each side

Meal One

1 x multivitamin

1 Whey Protein shake - with peanut butter and a banana

Bowl of Granola
NUTRITION FACTS
Calories: 561   Fat: 30.4 g   Carbs: 16.2 g   Protein: 28 g

Meal Two

2 Scoops of a 25 gram protein Whey Isolate shake

NUTRITION FACTS
Calories: 230   Fat: 20 g   Carbs: 10 g   Protein: 50 g

Meal Three

Two tins of Tuna
10 ounces

Vegetables/salad
1 cup
NUTRITION FACTS
Calories: 771   Fat: 33.2 g   Carbs: 17 g   Protein: 58 g

Meal Four

Full-Fat Cottage Cheese
2 cups
Almonds, Walnuts, Cashews – crushed up
2 ounces

NUTRITION FACTS
Calories: 752   Fat: 34 g Carb: 18 g   Protein: 52 g

The Total Protein intake is 182 grams of protein. I would have 2 scoops of protein plus Creatine after your workout making a grand total of 239.

This is a figure you can play with, add more, take away some etc.

25. Sunday - Rest

So we've made it to our rest day - well done for an epic workout!

So today is all about chilling, eating well, having your cheat meal - which is anything of your choice.

Meal One

1 x multivitamin
3-4 Whole Eggs
Bacon/Sausages or Quorn

Oats
1/4 cup with 1 tbsp. honey
NUTRITION FACTS
Calories: 561   Fat: 30.4 g   Carbs: 16.2 g   Protein: 22.1 g

Meal Two

2 Scoops of 25 gram protein Whey Isolate shake

NUTRITION FACTS
Calories: 230   Fat: 20 g   Carbs: 10 g   Protein: 50 g

Meal Three

Cheat Meal!

Meal Four

Full-Fat Cottage Cheese
2 cups
Almonds, Walnuts, or Cashews
2 ounces

NUTRITION FACTS
Calories: 752   Fat: 34 g Carb: 18 g   Protein: 52 g

26. Final Notes and Cheats

So we have reached the end of the training routine and your muscles should be aching. This is a good thing!

As I've said you may need to adjust your nutrition adding more protein, adding more carbs after training.

In terms of training you may struggle at first. I would reduce sets - not workouts. Keep to the schedule, keep working the muscles regularly and you will get results.

There are a number of cheats i use to maximize muscles gain in terms of supplements.

- A Pre and Post workout shake is a given - 25grams minimum.
- A scoop of BCAA's in 500ml of water pre-workout and something to sip. Again have this post workout.
- Creatine is a great as a post workout and fantastic to add muscle size.
- Fast-digesting carbs are also essential - oats and a large dollop of honey. Even an oatabix with honey. Or a carb drink like Waxy-maize.

So there we have it - have a go and enjoy the workouts!

If you'd like some brilliant Vegetarian food options here:

Vegetarian Bodybuilding Nutrition: How To Crack The Muscle Building Success Code With Vegetarian Bodybuilding Nutrition

24041604R00032

Printed in Great Britain
by Amazon